Dolphins

ERIK D. STOOPS, JEFFREY L. MARTIN & DEBBIE LYNNE STONE

Sterling Publishing Co., Inc.
New York

Library of Congress Cataloging-in-Publication Data

Stoops, Erik D., 1966–
    Dolphins / Erik D. Stoops, Jeffrey L. Martin & Debbie Lynne Stone.
        p.   cm.
    Includes index.
    Summary: Uses a question and answer format to reveal the life
cycle, lifestyle, and natural history of a wide variety of dolphin
species.
    ISBN 0-8069-0568-9
    1. Dolphins—Miscellanea—Juvenile literature.   [1. Dolphins—
Miscellanea.   2. Questions and answers.]   I. Martin, Jeffrey L.
II. Stone, Debbie Lynne.   III. Title.
QL737.C432S77   1996
599.5'3—dc20   95-46184
                                          CIP
                                          AC

Cover photograph: Common Dolphins by Dr. Bernd Würsig

Designed by Judy Morgan

1   3   5   7   9   10   8   6   4   2

First paperback edition published in 1998 by
Sterling Publishing Company, Inc.
387 Park Avenue South, New York, N.Y. 10016
© 1996 by Erik D. Stoops, Jeffrey L. Martin & Debbie Lynn Stone
Distributed in Canada by Sterling Publishing
% Canadian Manda Group, One Atlantic Avenue, Suite 105
Toronto, Ontario, Canada M6K 3E7
Distributed in Great Britain and Europe by Cassell PLC
Wellington House, 125 Strand, London WC2R 0BB, England
Distributed in Australia by Capricorn Link (Australia) Pty Ltd.
P.O. Box 6651, Baulkham Hills, Business Centre, NSW 2153, Australia
Printed in Hong Kong
All rights reserved

Sterling ISBN 0-8069-0568-9 Trade
0-8069-0569-7 Paper

CONTENTS

HOW DOLPHINS LIVE

Dolphins can usually be found in large groups. They help each other to hunt for food, watch for enemies, and care for their young. They are found throughout the world in more places than any other marine mammal.

◄**Dolphins are intelligent and inquisitive animals. This curious pair of Spotted Dolphins seems to be studying the scientist who took their picture.**

►**The Atlantic Salmon, a fish, has gills, so it can "breathe" underwater. It swims by moving its vertical tail from side to side.**

Is a dolphin a fish?

No. Dolphins look like fish at first glance, but they are actually mammals. Mammals are warm-blooded animals that bear their young live, and nurse them on their mother's milk. Dogs and cats are mammals, and so are people.

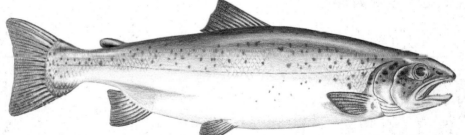

By Jeffrey L. Martin

By Kathleen Dudzinski

By Jeffrey L. Martin

◄**This Common Dolphin has lungs, so it must come to the water's surface to breathe air. It swims by moving its horizontal tail up and down.**

What is the difference between dolphins and porpoises?

Dolphins and porpoises are quite similar, but there are some important differences between them. Most dolphins have beak-like faces and pointed teeth. Porpoises have round faces and teeth shaped like little shovels.

By Thomas Jefferson

◄ Porpoises are smaller than most dolphins. They are also faster swimmers. This Harbor Porpoise became tangled in a gill net and drowned.

By Graham Worthy

▲ This is as much as you are likely to see of a live Harbor Porpoise. It does not jump out of the water nearly as often as dolphins do.

By NOAA: Keith Mullin

▲ The Bottlenose Dolphin was made famous by the 1960s TV show *Flipper*. Many people call this animal a porpoise, but it's really a dolphin. People get confused because these animals look so much alike.

What is the difference between dolphins and whales?

Dolphins and porpoises are actually small whales. There are thirteen whale families, each with its own distinct traits. They are all known as cetaceans (si-TA-shuns) or whales.

Cetaceans are divided into two major groups—baleen (buh-LEEN) whales and toothed whales. There are 11 baleen whale species, and most are very large. There are around 67 species of toothed whales. Dolphins and porpoises are included in this group.

By NOAA: Wayne Hoggard

◄ The largest toothed whale is the Sperm Whale. It grows to a length of nearly 52 feet (16m). Like most toothed whales, it uses its teeth to capture slippery fish and squid.

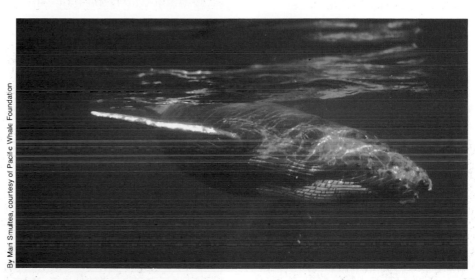

By Mari Smultea, courtesy of Pacific Whale Foundation

▲ The Humpback Whale is a baleen whale. It can grow to a length of 62 feet (19m) and weigh as much as 40 tons.

By Kathleen Dudzinski

◄ The Spotted Dolphin is what most people think of when they hear the word "dolphin." Each Spotted Dolphin's spots are different from all the others'. These dolphins can be told apart just by looking at their spots.

By Michael W. Newcomer

Why don't dolphins have fur?

Good question! Only mammals that live on land have fur. Seals and otters spend most of their time in the water, but they still come onto land now and then. Their fur coats protect their bodies from scrapes and help to keep them warm in and out of the water.

By Thomas Jefferson

▲ The Pilot Whale and the Bottlenose Dolphin look very different, but they are both dolphins. The Pilot Whale has no beak, but the Bottlenose Dolphin does.

▼ Unlike dolphins, seals and sea lions must leave the water to rest and to have their babies. You can easily see the fur of this young Harp Seal.

▲ Otters spend a lot of time preening and grooming themselves. Preening creates a layer of air under their fur that keeps them warm and dry when they swim in cold water.

What do dolphins look like?

Dolphins have fins and torpedo-shaped (streamlined) bodies. Their skin is very soft and smooth. Unlike most mammals, dolphins have no fur, although some do have tiny whiskers around their mouths.

By Graham Worthy

By Graham Worthy

▲ Besides whales and dolphins, manatees are the only mammals that stay in the water for all of their lives. They have very little hair and no hind legs. They are not related to whales and dolphins.

How fast can dolphins swim?

Most dolphins can swim faster than 25 miles (40km) per hour to escape a predator, or to catch fish. Normally, dolphins swim around 5 to 10 miles (8 to 16km) per hour. The fastest Olympic runners can run about 15mph (24km/h).

▶ The Dall's Porpoise is the fastest cetacean. It can swim as fast as 31 miles (50km) per hour!

By Jon Stern

▲ If a dolphin had fur, it would soon become soaked and useless. Dolphins can't leave the water to dry out, and their bodies are not flexible enough for them to preen.

By S. Mizroch, N.M.F.S., N.M.M.L.

Where do dolphins live?

Most dolphins live in saltwater. They are found in all oceans, from the shallow waters along the coast, to the deep waters of the open sea. Some dolphins spend their entire lives in fresh-water rivers and lakes.

▶ **The Spinner Dolphin gets its name from its habit of spinning as it leaps out of the water. It lives in the Indian, Pacific, and Atlantic oceans. It likes deep water, but sometimes comes close to shore.**

▶ **The Amazon River Dolphin lives in the Amazon and Orinoco rivers in South America. During the rainy season it swims into the flooded forests in search of food.**

By Barbara E. Curry

By Bernd Würsig

Do dolphins like warm or cold water?

Some dolphins live in the icy Arctic and Antarctic polar seas, but most inhabit warm tropical and temperate oceans. Temperate waters can be cool or warm, and their temperature usually changes with the seasons.

By R. Angliss

By NOAA: Wayne Hoggard

▲ The Spotted Dolphin can be found near land and in deep water. It prefers warm tropical waters.

▲ In the spring and summer, Belugas head for cold arctic waters in the north. These Belugas are swimming just off the coast near Point Barrow, Alaska.

By Peter Howorth

▲ The Common Dolphin lives in warm and temperate oceans around the world.

11

How many kinds of dolphins are there?

There are thirty-three ocean dolphins, five river dolphins, and six different kinds of porpoise.

What is the most common dolphin?

Many kinds of dolphins and porpoises are quite common. But their numbers are dropping because of pollution and fishing and hunting by humans.

By Bill Stevens

▲ **Bottlenose Dolphins are very common, especially in coastal waters. They like to follow** fishing boats to feed off scraps thrown overboard by fishermen.

By Thomas Jefferson

◀ **The Common Dolphin lives in warm oceans worldwide. Herds of these dolphins travel hundreds of miles, so they may be common in one place one year but quite scarce the next.**

What is the rarest dolphin?

Some of the rarest dolphins are the river dolphins of China and India. People use the river for their own needs, such as farming, building, and fishing. They don't think about the needs of these dolphins.

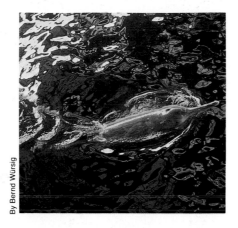

By Bernd Würsig

◄ The Beiji, or Chinese River, Dolphin is becoming very rare because the rivers where it lives are being polluted. It is now protected, but new laws may have come too late to save the Beiji.

What are river dolphins like?

River dolphins have chunky bodies, broad flippers, and wide tail fins (flukes). The fins on their backs (dorsal fins) are no more than humps or ridges. They have long thin beaks that they use to search for food in the river bottom. Unlike most dolphins, river dolphins can turn their heads. This is because their neck bones are not fused (grown together).

◄ The Amazon River Dolphin's eyes are tiny and not very useful, because it lives in cloudy water. It is one of the few dolphins that have special flattened teeth. It uses these to crush the thick-scaled fish that it eats.

By Jeffrey L. Martin

What is the biggest dolphin?

The Killer Whale, or Orca, is actually a large dolphin. An adult male can grow larger than 31 feet (9.5m) in length and weigh over eight tons (7200kg).

◄The straight dorsal fins of adult male Orcas are nearly six feet tall (1.8m). Females and calves have short, curved dorsal fins.

By Jeffrey L. Martin

▶Hector's Dolphin is one of the smallest dolphins. It doesn't grow much larger than 5½ feet (1.7m). It lives only in a small area around New Zealand.

By Bernd Würsig

Which are bigger — male or female dolphins?

Male dolphins are slightly bigger than females in most kinds of dolphins. But male Orcas are much larger than the females.

▶ **Female Orcas grow to a length of 22 feet (7m).**

By Mari A. Smultea

By Michael W. Newcomer

How big do porpoises become?

The smallest porpoise is the rare Vaquita, which only grows to a length of 4½ feet (1.4m). The other five porpoises are between 6 and 7 feet (1.8m–2.1m) long.

◀ **The little porpoise known as the Vaquita (va-KEET-a) lives in the Gulf of California. Only a few hundred of them are known to be alive today. Most pictures are of Vaquitas that have been found dead. Many drown in fishermen's nets.**

15

What is a group of dolphins called?

A gathering of dolphins can be called a herd, a school, a shoal, or a pod. Most dolphins swim in large herds. But river dolphins live in small herds, numbering from only 2 to 12 dolphins. Porpoises are rarely seen in pods of more than a dozen animals.

By Mari A. Smultea

◄A pod of Orcas is almost always a family group. There may be as many as 20 Orcas in a single pod, and they are all related. Pods of these animals stay together for 20 years and more.

By Bernd Würsig

▼By swimming in schools, dolphins can detect their enemies and find their food more easily. The more dolphins on the lookout, the better! Dolphins in the open ocean usually live in larger herds than the ones that live along a coast or in rivers.

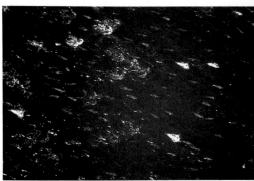

By NOAA Wayne Hoggard

▲Common Dolphins belong to some of the largest herds in the ocean. There may be 1,000 or more dolphins in a herd! They are not all related, and hundreds of dolphins may break away from the herd at any time.

By Gene Kent

▲This large school of Striped Dolphins was photographed from a research airplane. There may be 700 or more in a herd of Striped Dolphins.

Do different kinds of dolphins school together?

Yes! Many kinds of dolphins may be found in the same school. Dolphins even swim with large whales. Different kinds of dolphins are sometimes drawn together because they eat the same food.

▶ **Belugas and Bowhead Whales travel north together as summer approaches. The Bowheads, which are baleen whales, feed on tiny animals called plankton. Belugas eat crabs and fish.**

By R. Angliss

By Michael W. Newcomer

◀ **Pacific White-Sided Dolphins and Northern Right Whale Dolphins are often seen swimming together. Both of these dolphins live in the North Pacific.**

17

How far do dolphins travel?

Many dolphins travel hundreds of miles, following the fish they eat. Sometimes deep-sea dolphins, such as Spotted Dolphins, will swim into shallow coastal waters to feed.

By Bill Stevens

▲ Bottlenose Dolphins migrate toward the equator in the autumn. Then they travel back to cooler waters where they feed in spring. Although they live mainly along coasts, Bottlenose Dolphins have been sighted hundreds of miles from shore.

▶Northern Right Whale Dolphins head for the deep ocean in the summer, but stay closer to shore during the winter months.

By Michael W. Newcomer

Are dolphins smart?

Dolphins and porpoises are animals with large brains. They are curious and playful. These are signs of intelligence. Dolphins play with their food, with seaweed, with each other, with other animals, and even with boats. Bottlenose Dolphins have been found to understand words and Rough-Toothed Dolphins are also known to understand commands.

▲ Bottlenose Dolphins are famous for their playfulness. This one is flipping a flounder it has caught into the air.

▲ A Bottlenose Dolphin can turn just about anything into a toy. Here a jellyfish is the object of its attention.

By Dagmar C. Fertl

By Dagmar C. Fertl

▲ Dolphins like to ride the wave at the bow (front) of a boat, or just race alongside. They leap out of the water and appear to be watching people riding in the boat. Dolphins also bow-ride in front of large whales.

▲ Dolphins are very smart and can be taught many different tasks, such as wearing test equipment like these floats.

By Bernd Würsig

▲ The Dusky Dolphin is well known for its energetic flips as it leaps out of the water. Duskies will make up to 50 leaps in a row.

Why do dolphins jump out of the water?

Dolphins jump, or breach, to confuse and herd fish that they are chasing, or to travel faster and see farther. They also breach to loosen tiny animals that cling to their sensitive skin. Some dolphins jump so dramatically that they seem to be doing it just for fun!

20

By Bernd Würsig

▲Dusky Dolphins like to chase each other. Once one starts jumping, it gets others started.

By Mari A. Smultea

Before you know it, hundreds of Duskies are churning up the sea!

◀To see an Orca breaching is truly a memorable sight. The largest of all dolphins, the Orca makes a huge splash. The crashing noise can be heard for miles underwater. Some scientists think the Orca is saying, "Watch out everybody, I'm here!"

By Kathleen Dudzinski

Do dolphins ever get sick?

Yes. Like all other living things, dolphins do get sick or become injured. Dental disease, broken bones, and tumors are a few of the conditions dolphins must live with. Man-made chemicals, such as pesticides, end up in the bodies of dolphins, and this can make them sick and die.

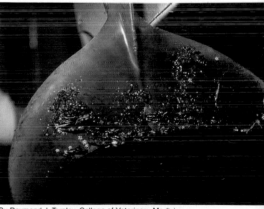
By Raymond J. Tarpley, College of Veterinary Medicine, Texas A&M University

Are dolphins really smiling?

The muscles in your face lie just below your skin. They allow you to smile or frown or scowl. A dolphin's facial muscles are buried beneath a thick layer of blubber. The jaw bones, blubber, and skin shape the dolphin's face. Even when it is afraid or angry, a dolphin still appears to be smiling.

▲ Like other dolphins, this Spotted Dolphin cannot change the expression on its face to show how it is feeling. It appears to be smiling, but it is not really.

How long do dolphins live?

Most dolphins live to be 25 to 30 years old. Orcas can live to be 80 years old.

▲ Just as dogs get ticks and fleas, dolphins also have parasites. The flukes of this Bottlenose Dolphin are covered with barnacles.

THE DOLPHIN'S BODY

Just about the time the dinosaurs disappeared, certain land mammals began to venture into the ocean. No one knows why. Perhaps the land had become too crowded. Or maybe these animals filled the space left open by ancient fish-like reptiles that became extinct along with the dinosaurs. Whatever the reason, these mammals went on to become the whales and dolphins we know today.

◄ **Dolphins are beautiful, agile animals. They are excellent swimmers. Their bodies have evolved in many ways to make them perfect for life in the sea.**

By Jeffrey L. Martin

By Kathleen Dudzinski

▲ **The Longnose Porpoise is an ancient porpoise. It looked a lot like the dolphins of today, but it had a much longer beak. It lived about 12 million years ago.**

Do dolphins have any relatives on land?

Believe it or not, the dolphin's closest land relatives are probably pigs, cows, and deer! Dolphins evolved in the ocean while hoofed animals evolved on land.

23

How long ago did the first dolphins live?

Dolphins and porpoises, as we know them today, first swam the seas around 12 million years ago. They were similar, but not identical, to the modern animals.

What colors are dolphins?

The most common dolphin colors are black, white, light grey, and blue-grey. All dolphins have one or more of these colors on their bodies. A few dolphin species also have yellow, tan, and even pink. Some dolphins have spots or stripes.

By Richard A. Rowlett

◄ The Common Dolphin has graceful color patterns of grey, tan, black, and white. This animal has washed up on the beach. It's not as easy to see its beautiful markings when it is swimming in the water.

By Dagmar C. Fertl

▲ The Striped Dolphin is named for the black stripe that runs from its head to its tail. This animal is sometimes mistaken for the Common Dolphin, because it has similar markings.

Official U.S. Navy Photograph

◄ Adult Belugas are pure white. Belugas are grey when they are born, but get lighter in color as they get older.

By Mari A. Smultea

▲ The Orca is a beautiful animal! It is boldly marked in black and white. The white patch just behind its eye sets it apart from all other dolphins.

What does "warm-blooded" mean?

Being warm-blooded means having the ability to control body temperature. Mammals create body heat by changing food into heat energy.

▶ **These Belugas live in very cold water. They often have to swim through fields of pack ice. Keeping their bodies at a warm temperature is important.**

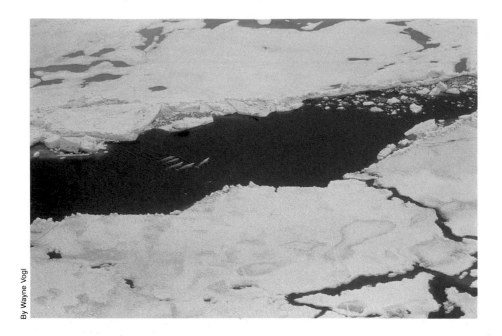

By Wayne Vogl

How warm is a dolphin's body?

Deep within a dolphin's body its temperature is normally 96° to 98°F (35° to 36.9°C). Its outer body temperature is usually cooler than this. Your body temperature is 98.6°F (37.3°C).

▼ **This diagram shows how a dolphin looks on the inside.**

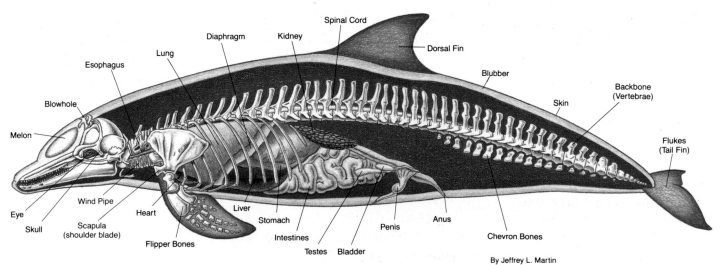

Spinal Cord
Diaphragm
Kidney
Dorsal Fin
Lung
Esophagus
Blubber
Backbone (Vertebrae)
Blowhole
Skin
Melon
Flukes (Tail Fin)
Eye
Wind Pipe
Liver
Anus
Heart
Skull
Stomach
Penis
Chevron Bones
Scapula (shoulder blade)
Intestines
Flipper Bones
Testes   Bladder

By Jeffrey L. Martin

26

How do dolphins keep warm?

Heat is lost in water very quickly. To keep heat from escaping, the dolphin has a thick layer of fat known as blubber just beneath its skin. Blubber holds in warmth, and keeps out the cold. The dolphin also has special blood vessels that absorb heat and carry it back to the center of the dolphin's body.

▲ Since cetaceans do not have fur to keep them warm, their blubber does the job. Blubber is especially important in the cold North Pacific, where this Dall's Porpoise lives.

▲ Dolphins do not need to breathe very often, so they don't lose much heat from breathing out. When you see your breath on cold days, that's a sign that heat is escaping. These are Risso's Dolphins.

Can dolphins get too warm?

A dolphin's body actually can overheat if it swims fast for a long period of time. Overheating can be dangerous to a dolphin, because it can become exhausted and drown.

How do dolphins cool off?

Fortunately, dolphins have a number of ways to cool off. To prevent overheating, the dolphin's body automatically allows more blood to flow to its skin and fins. This helps shed excess body heat into the water.

27

How do dolphins breathe?

Dolphins have lungs and breathe air just like people do. They have to hold their breath when they swim or dive underwater. Strong muscles keep their blowholes shut tight so water cannot get in.

▼ **This is what a Bottlenose Dolphin's blowhole looks like when it is shut.**

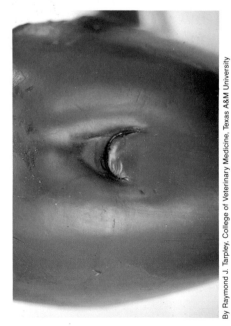

By Raymond J. Tarpley, College of Veterinary Medicine, Texas A&M University

By Mari A. Smultea courtesy of Pacific Whale Foundation

▲ **The Pilot Whale is an excellent diver! It can dive as deep as 3,000 feet (900m) and hold its breath for at least ten minutes.**

How can a dolphin hold its breath for so long?

Good question! Like all animals, dolphins need oxygen to survive. But dolphins and other whales have some special abilities that other animals do not. They are able to send oxygen-rich blood to only the most important parts of the body, the brain and heart. When dolphins dive, they store oxygen in their blood, muscles, and small blood vessels called retia (pronounced REE-sha). Dolphins can also slow down their hearts so they use their oxygen supply more slowly than other animals do.

By Kathleen Dudzinski

Do dolphins have bones?

Yes, but since a dolphin spends its entire life in the water, its bones are lighter and more "spongy" than those of land mammals. They are filled with fat and oil. There are only two tiny bones where the hip bones and hind legs used to be.

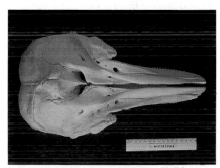

By Raymond J. Tarpley, College of Veterinary Medicine, Texas A&M University

How does a dolphin keep from drowning?

Even when a dolphin is swimming very slowly, it comes to the surface for only a moment. It needs to know the exact instant its blowhole has broken the surface so that it doesn't breathe in water and drown. A dolphin's skin is extremely sensitive around the blowhole. It can feel the differences between the water and the air.

▲ Dolphins are also voluntary breathers. This means *they decide* when they want to breathe. Our brains automatically keep us breathing whether we are awake or sleeping, or if we should faint.

▲ This is a top view of the skull of an Atlantic White-Sided Dolphin. The two big holes on top are the nostrils (the "blowhole"). In all other mammals, the nostrils are at the tip of the nose.

What kind of fins do dolphins have?

All dolphins have two flippers and a tail fin. Most dolphins also have a fin on their backs. Another name for the tail fin is "flukes." The dolphin uses its flukes to push itself forward in the water.

▶ **This is the tail fin of a Spotted Dolphin.**

By Kathleen Dudzinski

By Dagmar C. Fertl

▲ You can easily see the fins on the backs of these Bottlenose Dolphins. The fin on a dolphin's back is called its "dorsal" fin. Its dorsal fin keeps it from rolling from side to side as it swims.

By Thomas Jefferson

▲The Northern Right Whale Dolphin is one of the few dolphins that has no dorsal fin.

▶ The flippers are located just behind the head of this Bottlenose Dolphin. It uses its flippers to steer right or left and up or down.

By NOAA Keith D. Mullin

What are the dolphin's flippers like?

Despite the dolphin's outward appearance, it has kept some of the traits of its land-dwelling ancestors. Its flipper is a lot like your arm. Nearly all of the bones are there, from the shoulder blade down to the fingertips, although their shapes are different. A dolphin cannot bend its "elbows." It can only move its flippers at the shoulders.

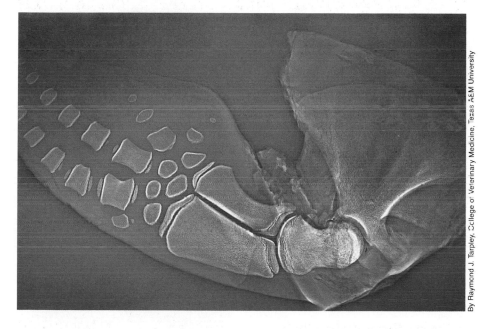

By Raymond J. Tarpley, College of Veterinary Medicine, Texas A&M University

▲ In this X-ray, you can see all the bones in a dolphin's flipper. They have become flattened so that the flipper can "cut" through the water. Dolphins have more "finger" bones than their land relatives.

▶ The shiny smoothness of this Northern Right Whale Dolphin's skin helps it slip effortlessly through the water.

What is the dolphin's tail fin like?

Since a dolphin's flippers are its "arms," you might think that its tail fin is its legs. But it's not. There are no bones supporting a dolphin's tail fin. Instead, tough strands of tissue called ligaments (LIG-a-mints) stiffen the tail fin, and attach it firmly to the tail vertebrae. You have ligaments holding your arm bones together at your elbow.

What does a dolphin's skin feel like?

A dolphin's skin is soft and extremely smooth. It has no pores, wrinkles, or follicles (hair roots), except for a few on its beak.

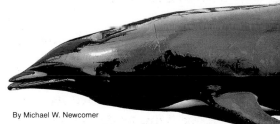

By Michael W. Newcomer

31

THE DOLPHIN'S SENSES

Life in a watery world is vastly different from life on land. The information dolphins get from their surroundings is unlike any you get from day to day. Their senses have developed in many surprising ways to meet the demands of life in the sea.

◄Dolphins have very sensitive skin. They often touch each other while they are swimming. This is one way they let each other know if all is well.

How well do dolphins see?

Unlike your eyes, which need a diving mask to see clearly underwater, dolphins' eyes are built to see clearly in the water *and* in the air. They have a strong lens that can change shape to focus light. The dolphin's eyes also adjust very well to dim and bright light.

By Mari A. Smultea

◄One of these Orcas is spy-hopping. The other is looking and listening underwater.

Can dolphins see colors?

Yes, but no one is sure how many colors. Some dolphins tested could tell red and yellow from other colors. We also don't know how many species have color vision, because not that many have been tested.

By Kathleen Dudzinski

Can dolphins close their eyes?

Dolphins have upper and lower eyelids. Their eyes close when they sleep. Dolphins also close their eyes to protect them from objects in the water.

▶ **If you look closely, you can see this Bottlenose Dolphin's eyelids. Like all dolphins and porpoises, the Bottlenose has no eyelashes.**

Print By Terry Christopher

Do dolphins talk to each other?

Dolphin language sounds to us like clicks, squeaks, pops, and whistles. Scientists are trying to figure out what all these sounds mean. Dolphins warn each other when an enemy gets too close, or if food is nearby. But only dolphins know exactly what they are saying!

Do dolphins have ears?

One look at a dolphin and you can tell that it does not have an outer ear like you do, but it *does* have an inner ear and it can hear very well.

By Mari A. Smultea

◀ **Each pod of Orcas has its own language. Scientists can tell one pod from another just by listening to them.**

What can dolphins hear?

Dolphins can hear sounds that are too high-pitched for us, as well as sounds we *can* hear. They can hear other dolphins, whales, fishes, and boats. But more importantly, they can hear their own echoes. To a dolphin, echoes are as important as fins! *Without echoes, a dolphin would not be able to survive.*

▲ **Finding food, avoiding enemies, navigating — a dolphin can do all this and more just by using echoes.**

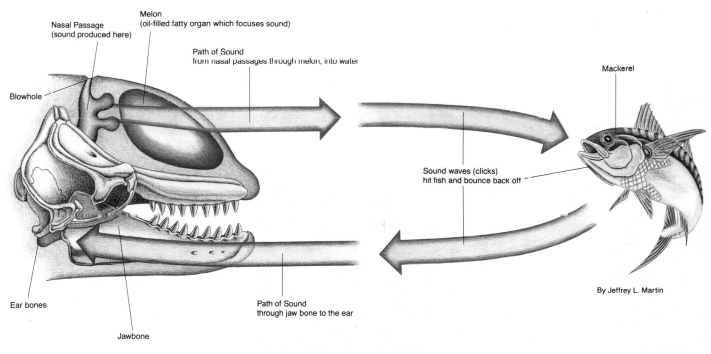

Nasal Passage
(sound produced here)

Melon
(oil-filled fatty organ which focuses sound)

Path of Sound
from nasal passages through melon, into water

Mackerel

Blowhole

Sound waves (clicks)
hit fish and bounce back off

Ear bones

Path of Sound
through jaw bone to the ear

Jawbone

By Jeffrey L. Martin

▲ **This diagram shows how a dolphin uses echolocation.**

How does a dolphin use echoes?

The dolphin sends out clicking sounds into the water. If these clicks come back, it means they bounced off an object. The dolphin then sends out thousands of short rapid clicks to find out the size, shape, and location of the object. The dolphin can tell if it's a fish or a squid or a shark or a boat without even seeing it! This is called echolocation (EK-o-lo-KA-tion) or sonar.

What is stranding?

Dolphins sometimes swim into very shallow water, and become stuck on the beach when the tide goes out. This is called stranding. If the animals are unable to return to the water or receive help, they will die.

▶ **Sometimes shallow water confuses dolphins' sonar, and they strand themselves on the beach. This is a Risso's Dolphin.**

▶ **Besides using echolocation to find underwater landmarks, dolphins navigate by sensing and following magnetic patterns in the Earth.**

How far can dolphins hear?

Dolphins can echolocate over a distance of at least 2,500 feet (800m). That is about 10 times as far as they can see in the water.

▶ **Sick or dying dolphins enter shallow water to rest. But occasionally healthy *herds* of dolphins, like Pilot Whales, also strand. This is probably because they become confused by distorted magnetic patterns in the Earth.**

By Kathleen Dudzinski

By Graham Worthy

By Thomas Jefferson

What can dolphins feel?

Dolphins have very sensitive skin. They can detect very small changes in pressure around their bodies while swimming. They can also adjust their body shape to become more streamlined.

By Kathleen Dudzinski

By Thomas Jefferson

▲As these Spotted Dolphins play, they constantly touch each other with their fins, snouts, and bodies.

◄Pacific White-Sided Dolphins, like other dolphins, rely mainly on their excellent hearing and eyesight. It doesn't matter that they have no sense of smell.

Can a dolphin smell?

When, over millions of years, the dolphin's blowhole moved from the tip of its nose to the top of its head, it lost its sense of smell. Since it is holding its breath most of the time, a dolphin hasn't any use for a sense of smell.

Can dolphins taste their food?

Dolphins do have a sense of taste. They can tell if something is sweet, sour, bitter, or salty. Dolphins can also tell if a fish is fresh, and they will not eat rotten fish.

EATING HABITS

Dolphins have to eat a lot of food. They need food energy to keep warm and to swim. But they don't need to eat all the time, because they can store energy in their body fat. Dolphins "fatten up" when there is plenty to eat, and live off their fat when there isn't much food to be found.

◄These hungry Orcas are patrolling the water's edge for sea lions. Orcas sometimes even slide onto the beach to catch sea lions right on land!

By S. Mizroch, N.M.F.S., N.M.M.L.

◄The Dall's Porpoise will eat as much as 33 pounds (15kg) per day. That's about one-ninth of its body weight.

What do dolphins eat?

Dolphins such as the Bottlenose eat fish, squid, and jellyfish. River dolphins eat fish, crabs, and clams. Killer Whales, the largest dolphins, also feed on seals, sea lions, penguins, sharks, sea turtles, other dolphins and whales.

How much food do dolphins eat?

Dolphins are able to eat plenty of food. A Killer Whale was once found with 13 dolphins and 14 seals in its stomach!

By Bernd Würsig

By S. Mizroch, N.M.F.S. N.M.M.L.

▲ The Pacific White-Sided Dolphin likes to eat squid and anchovies. It eats about 20 pounds (9kg) in a day.

Do dolphins chew their food?

No, dolphins swallow their food whole.

▶Dolphin teeth are built for catching and holding on to slippery fish that are small enough to swallow whole.

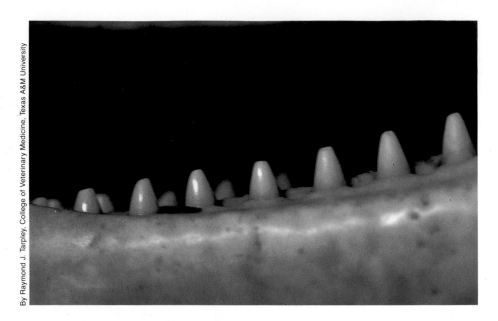

By Raymond J. Tarpley, College of Veterinary Medicine, Texas A&M University

By Raymond J. Tarpley, College of Veterinary Medicine, Texas A&M University

What do a dolphin's teeth look like?

Most dolphins have pointed, cone-shaped teeth. Some species have sharp, curved teeth, while porpoises' teeth are shaped like little shovels.

◀This is the mouth of a baby Bottlenose Dolphin. Its teeth have yet to pop out through its gums. It does not need them yet, because it is still nursing.

Do dolphins get two sets of teeth as people do?

Unlike people, dolphins get only one set of teeth. If a tooth is lost or worn down, a new tooth does not grow in to replace it.

▶ **You can easily see this Northern Right Whale Dolphin's sharp, pointy teeth. As this dolphin gets older, its teeth will wear down, and become blunt.**

By Michael W. Newcomer

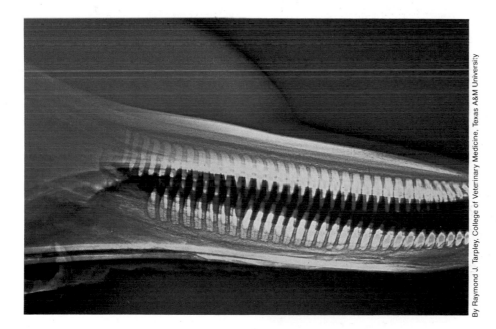

By Raymond J. Tarpley, College of Veterinary Medicine, Texas A&M University

How many teeth do dolphins have?

Some dolphins have many teeth, while others have very few. Spinner Dolphins have the most, about 250 or more. Risso's Dolphins have only 14. Most dolphins have between 100 and 160 teeth. Most porpoises have about 100 teeth.

◀ **This X-ray shows how a Bottlenose Dolphin's teeth are set in its head.**

How do dolphins get their food?

Dolphins get their food in a variety of ways. Orcas tip ice floes (large drifting chunks of ice) and grab penguins and seals that slip from the ice. Orcas also hunt in packs, attacking and eating even the largest whales. Dusky Dolphins work together to herd fish into a tightly packed group near the surface, so the fish can't escape. Then the dolphins charge into the school. The fish panic and are easy to catch.

▲ Many kinds of dolphins herd fish the way these Duskies do.

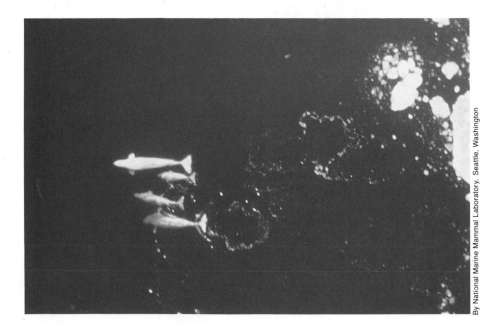

◄ Besides eating fish like other dolphins, Belugas also eat crabs and other crustaceans. They find them in shallow ocean and river beds.

42

By Mari A. Smultea

▲ This Orca is holding its head high out of the water to have a look around. This is known as spy-hopping.

Why do dolphins spy-hop?

Dolphins spy-hop to look around for food on the surface of the water, on ice floes, or on a nearby beach.

Do dolphins drink water?

Dolphins do not need to drink water, but they may swallow some as they feed. They get their water from the fish they eat, and from the blubber in their bodies.

Do dolphins get fat?

When food is abundant, a dolphin's layer of blubber gets thicker. When food becomes scarce, the blubber gets thinner. Then the dolphin lives off its fat. Dolphins don't really have a chance to get fat, because swimming is very good exercise.

DOLPHIN REPRODUCTION

Because dolphins are marine animals, much of their lives is a mystery to us. Scientists around the world are trying to answer questions about the dolphin's reproductive habits. Here are some of the fascinating things we do know about dolphin reproduction.

◀ **The mother dolphin rarely leaves its baby's side. From the time it is born, the calf is nursed and nurtured by its mother. Other female dolphins (called "aunts") baby-sit when the mother feeds.**

How can you tell male and female dolphins apart?

It is nearly impossible to tell male and female dolphins apart without looking very closely at the underside of their bodies where their reproductive organs are tucked away in slits to make swimming easier. Male dolphins have a separate anal slit, while females have a pair of small mammary slits on either side of the genital slit.

How do dolphins court each other?

Bottlenose Dolphins touch each other frequently with their flippers, flukes, and snout. They nuzzle each other and swim close together. This sometimes lasts longer than an hour. Courting behavior does not always lead to mating.

How do they mate?

Male and female dolphins swim belly to belly when they mate. Mating usually does not take very long, only about 30 seconds.

▼ **Most dolphins mate all year round. These Bottlenose Dolphins are courting.**

By Dagmar C. Fertl

By Kathleen Dudzinski

◄This is a rare photo of dolphins mating in the wild.

By Gene Kent

Where do dolphins mate?

Where dolphins mate depends on the species and where it lives. Since dolphins follow the fish they eat, mating could take place anywhere the dolphins' food is found. Dolphins may go where there is no danger from predators, such as shallow lagoons. Unlike many other dolphins, the Dusky Dolphin mates underwater at about 30 feet (10m).

▶ Before this Pilot Whale was born its mother carried it in her womb for 16 months.

How long is a dolphin pregnant?

The length of time a dolphin is pregnant is called the "gestation" (jes-TA-shun) period. Most dolphins have a gestation period of between 9 to 12 months. But some dolphins take longer.

By Mari A. Smultea, courtesy of Pacific Whale Foundation

By Jeffrey L. Martin

How are dolphin babies born?

Like all cetaceans, dolphin babies are born in the water. Among mammals this is very rare. The only other mammals that bear their babies in the water are the manatees, which are not related to whales.

▲ This Bottlenose Dolphin is having a baby. Most baby dolphins are born tail first. Baby dolphins that are born head first may drown before they are free of their mother.

What are dolphin babies called?

Baby dolphins are called calves. Older calves are known as juveniles.

►Newborn calves, such as this baby Bottlenose Dolphin, are called neonates (NEE-o-nates).

By Bill Stevens

47

How many calves do dolphins have?

Most dolphins have only one calf. Sometimes twins are born, but usually only one of them survives.

▶This mother Pilot Whale keeps her calf close to her to protect it from predators. She will also help it to swim to the surface to breathe.

By Mari A. Smultea courtesy of Pacific Whale Foundation

Do babies look different from adults?

Calves look very much like their parents, except that they are smaller. With some species, the young dolphins' colors or markings are different from those of their parents.

By Michael W. Newcomer

By Kathleen Dudzinski

◀Baby Spotted Dolphins are born without spots. Their spots appear as the calves get older.

▲ This Common Dolphin calf is lighter in color than its parents, and its beak is shorter. If you look carefully, you can see the stripes on its body.

48

How big is a calf when it is born?

The size of a calf depends on its species. Some of the largest calves are Orcas. Some of the smaller calves are Common and Spotted Dolphins.

▶Baby Orcas are about 7 feet (2.2m) long when they are born. They can weigh as much as 300 pounds (136kg). That's as large as the adults of some dolphin species!

◀When this Spotted Dolphin was a baby, it measured about 3 feet (9m).

By Dagmar C. Fertl

▲Scientists have found that many offspring stay with their mothers throughout their lives. This is a mother Bottlenose Dolphin and her calf.

Do dolphins make good parents?

Females are excellent parents. They will stay with their calf for at least the first year of its life. The role of the male in child rearing usually ends with mating, but they do occasionally baby-sit.

▶This Spinner Dolphin calf stays very close to its mother all the time. It will even jump out of the water when she does.

By Mari A. Smultea

▲This adult male Orca is most likely the son of one of the females in the pod. Females are called cows. Males are called bulls. A bull may leave the pod for a short time to mate with a cow from another pod. The entire pod centers around the females, which do not leave the group.

By Michael W. Newcomer

By Michael W. Newcomer

▲ Baby dolphins and porpoises nurse most of the day.

Do calves nurse?

All mammals nurse and dolphins are no exception. The females feed their calves a nutritious milk that is high in fat. The mother pumps the milk from nipples in her mammary slits into the baby's mouth.

How often do calves nurse?

Since the calves must keep going to the surface for air, they only nurse for a few seconds at a time. Some reports state that calves nurse every 15 minutes.

How old is a calf when it stops nursing?

Calves nurse for a year or more, but they may start snacking on fish by the time they are six months old. This supplements their diet as they learn to catch their own food.

Are dolphins good baby-sitters?

Yes, and the cooperative effort of these "aunts" allows the mother dolphin time to eat without keeping a constant watch over her calf. They may even help the mother push the newborn up to the surface for its first breath.

▶ **While adult females take turns watching one another's calves, younger females also spend time playing with the baby.**

Do baby dolphins cry?

No. Dolphins do make sounds to communicate, but they do not cry, as human children do. Since a dolphin's eyes are open underwater most of the time, the animal has mucous secretions that help keep its eyes moist and protects them against saltwater. These secretions look like tears, but they are not.

By Kathleen Dudzinski

How long does it take for a calf to grow up?

Becoming an adult dolphin means being old enough to have babies. Different species mature at different ages. In most species females mature earlier than males.

By Dagmar C. Fertl

▲Striped Dolphins are old enough to have babies when they are 6 to 9 years old. They grow to around 7 feet (2.1m) in length.

▶This Bottlenose Dolphin is about 6 years old. It will be considered an adult when it is between 8 and 10 years of age.

By Dagmar C. Fertl

Do baby dolphins talk to their mothers?

Yes, moms and calves "talk" with each other using squeaks, clicks, and whistles. Much of their communication is through touching and rubbing, just like other animals, including humans.

SELF-DEFENSE

The life of a dolphin is not always fun. It must watch out for its enemies. It must also feed itself and find partners for mating. All of these activities require a dolphin to run or to defend itself from time to time.

◄Dolphins live in groups. They must cooperate in order to survive. Much of their survival depends on their ability to defend themselves.

What are the dolphin's enemies?

Sharks and Killer Whales eat dolphins. Dolphins are also hunted or accidentally killed by humans. Many dolphins die in tuna nets. Sadly, it is the dolphins that alert fishermen to the tuna to begin with. Tuna fishermen look for dolphins to find tuna.

►Dolphins and tuna like to eat the same food. When they find a huge school of herring or sardines, they feed together. If the ocean's surface is churning with hundreds of dolphins, chances are good that tuna are around. Spinner Dolphins, like these, are more likely to be caught with the tuna than any other species.

By Michael W. Newcomer

By Kathleen Dudzinski

◄ This dolphin is pulling fish from a fishing net. This one is not in danger, but thousands drown each year in tuna nets and driftnets.

▼ The dorsal fin of this Orca was injured by a boat propeller. Boaters should take special care if they know there are cetaceans in the area.

By Dagmar C. Fertl

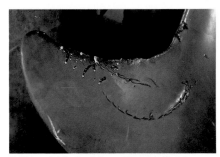

By Raymond J. Tarpley, College of Veterinary Medicine, Texas A&M University

▲ This Bottlenose Dolphin's dorsal fin has been bitten by a shark.

By Thomas Jefferson

56

How do dolphins protect themselves?

Dolphins protect themselves by swimming in schools. A whole school of dolphins can detect its enemies better than only one animal can.

Do dolphins fight among themselves?

Yes. Males fight each other for mating rights and for the best feeding opportunities. They lunge and slap at each other with their flukes, clap their jaws, and even bite. They threaten each other by shaking their bodies. They also sometimes fight with females and their calves.

By Bill Stevens

▲ The deeper the water, the greater the dolphins' need to form large schools. There is nowhere to hide, so these Spotted Dolphins must be able to outrun predators.

▼ Male Narwhals may fight for hours to mate with a female. They have long tusks that they use as weapons. Tusk wounds can be deadly.

▼ Normally, it's only the male Narwhal that has a tusk, but some females have tusks as well. The tusk is actually a tooth. It can grow as long as 10 feet (3m).

By David C. Pfeiffer

By Adam Ravetch

Do dolphins take care of each other?

Yes. Dolphins can become sick or get injured now and then. This can weaken them, so that they need help from their companions. Dolphins help each other because they need to be strong as a group.

▲ **If a dolphin is sick or injured, its companions will swim closely and even push it to the surface to breathe. When this dolphin gets well, it will help others, in return.**

58

By Mari A. Smultea courtesy of Pacific Whale Foundation

How do dolphins sleep?

Sleeping is easy for an animal living on land, because it does not need to worry about breathing. A dolphin has to deal with the problem of getting the sleep it needs, while staying awake enough to keep from drowning.

▲ Dolphin sleep is a little like cat-napping. Each half of the dolphin's brain takes turns sleeping. The other half makes sure that the dolphin gets to the surface to breathe. This way of sleeping also helps dolphins to stay alert to predators, such as sharks.

DOLPHINS AND PEOPLE

Since prehistoric times, dolphins have played many roles in the lives of humans. Ancient Scandinavians, who depended on dolphins and whales for food, painted pictures of them onto huge boulders by the sea. Dolphins were worshipped as gods in Greek and Roman mythology. Today, dolphins are in trouble. Not all people respect them, or the rivers and oceans in which they live.

◄**Like many wild creatures, dolphins shy away when approached by humans. But dolphins do learn to trust humans if they are slowly introduced to people and shown respect.**

Are dolphins friendly?

Yes. Stories dating back nearly 2,000 years tell of dolphins befriending people. Modern-day reports tell of dolphins rescuing people who are in trouble in the water. They are known to have pulled divers away from waters where sharks were gathering.

By Michael W. Newcomer

▲**Bottlenose Dolphins are probably the friendliest species. They are curious about people, and seem to understand that people are curious about them.**

By Peter Howorth

Why are dolphins killed?

Dolphins and fishermen often fish in the same place. Dolphins become trapped in the fishermen's gill-nets. Dolphins are sometimes deliberately killed because they are seen as thieves that steal fish. But fishermen catch many more fish than dolphins do. Then they blame the dolphins because there are fewer fish to catch.

Why are dolphins hunted?

In some countries dolphins are hunted for food. The parts of the dolphin that people do not eat are ground up and used in animal food and fertilizer. The skulls of dolphins contain a high-quality oil, which has been used to oil delicate instruments such as watches and clocks. Blubber oil is used to tan leather.

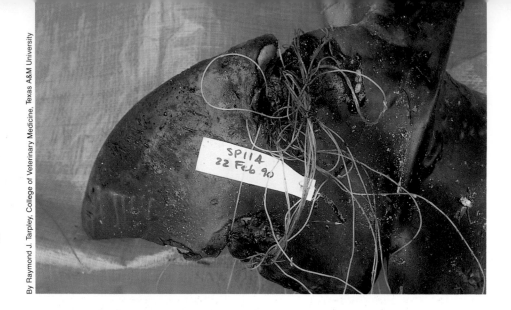

▲ This dolphin drowned as a result of being caught in a drift-net. A drift-net is a large, fine-stranded net that drifts over a wide area of the sea. You can see that the net has cut into its flukes.

▼ Orcas are among the deadliest hunters in the sea, and the largest meat-eaters living today. They eat a variety of animals, including sharks, seals, and large whales. Yet for some reason, they will not knowingly attack people.

By Kathleen Dudzinski

▲ Some dolphins become accustomed to people if they are around them enough.

These Spotted Dolphins did not run away from the divers photographing them. They became curious and approached the scientists to see what they were doing.

What other ways do people hurt dolphins?

Humans pollute the rivers, gulfs, and oceans where dolphins and porpoises live. Factories and sewers dump their wastes into the water. Pollution gets into the bodies of dolphins and porpoises. This makes them sick and many of them die.

By Michael W. Newcomer

▲ The Vaquita is endangered because of overfishing and pollution. It lives only in the northern Gulf of California. If its home is polluted further, it will have no place to live.

►Although the Striped Dolphin is considered common by scientists, it may become endangered. This animal was found dead on a beach.

By Thomas Jefferson

What can I do to protect dolphins?

You can study and learn about these wonderful animals and join marine mammal organizations that help protect dolphins, such as the World Wildlife Fund. Write to your government officials to pressure them to end the use of gill-nets and drift-nets. There are many organizations to write to, including Earthtrust in Hawaii, the American Cetacean Society in Sacramento, California, and the International Wildlife Coalition in Maine. There are also the Whale Rescue Centre in Australia and World Society for the Protection of Animals in the United Kingdom.

What is the World Wildlife Fund?

This organization is instrumental in raising the most money for conservation projects. It has greatly helped dolphin conservation projects worldwide, particularly for endangered river dolphins.

By Thomas Jefferson

▶**These dolphins were found stranded on the beach at Matagorda Bay, which is on the coast of the Gulf of Mexico. Unfortunately, they could not be saved.**

What can I do if I find a stranded dolphin?

Keep onlookers and dogs at a distance to keep the dolphin calm. Notify the police, lifeguard, the local stranding network, or the Coast Guard as soon as possible. Do not push the dolphin back into the water. The dolphin's skin, flippers, and blowhole can be injured by the sand. If you have others with you, check the dolphin to see if it's alive. Stand in front of the dolphin's head so you won't get hurt by its thrashing tail. Make sure its blowhole is clear so it can breathe.

▶**Keep the dolphin damp, cool, and calm by carefully laying wet towels or seaweed on its body. Try to keep the dolphin shaded so it will not become too hot. If the dolphin is dead, it is still important to notify officials.**

By Terry Christopher

66

By Terry Christopher

By Terry Christopher

▲ This baby Risso's Dolphin was transferred to a small holding tank. Proper medications were given by staff veterinarians so the animal wouldn't go into shock.

▲ The veterinarian was able to save this Risso's Dolphin.

By Dagmar Fertl

◄ Scientists are taking a small blubber sample from this dolphin to look for man-made poisons and pollutants. They hope to find out who is polluting the ocean, so that dolphins can be better protected.

How do scientists study dolphins?

Scientists use a variety of equipment to study dolphins. X-ray, surgery, and medical tests are used to find out what makes dolphins sick, and how they may be cured. Special underwater recording equipment helps scientists to analyze the complex sounds dolphins make.

▶ The Oregon II is a National Oceanic and Atmospheric Administration research vessel. It has living quarters and laboratory and electronic equipment. Scientists on board track dolphin herds with sonar. They spot dolphins using these powerful binoculars, which they call "big eyes."

NOAA Wayne Hoggard

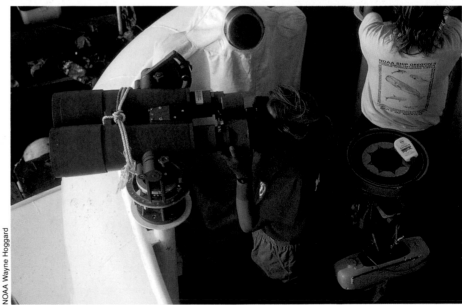

NOAA Wayne Hoggard

◄This airplane is called a Twin Otter. It can easily survey large areas of the ocean for dolphins. When it finds dolphins, it calls the research ship by radio.

◄On this dolphin's fin, scientists mounted a small radio transmitter to track the animal's movements throughout the day.

What does "Dolphin Safe" mean?

"Dolphin Safe" means that commercial tuna fishermen did not trap the dolphins that feed with tuna while trapping the tuna.

If I wanted to study dolphins, what would I be?

There are a number of jobs and careers available. A marine biologist might study the animal's eating habits. A cetacean biologist might study reproduction or a cetologist might study the communication and behavior of the many dolphin and whale species.

By Terry Christopher

▲ **People naturally try to help dolphins in trouble. This Pygmy Killer Whale was stranded and weak. These scientists and volunteers are helping it back into the water.**

Where can I go to see dolphins?

Many aquariums display dolphins. Also whale-watching tours are a great way to view these mammals.

▼ **Fishing nets kill thousands of marine mammals, like this Melon Headed Whale, each year.**

By Graham Worthy

◄ **The science team has taken the Pygmy Killer Whale to a holding pen until it is well enough to set free.**

By Thomas Jefferson

What is the IWC?

The IWC is the International Whaling Commission, formed in 1946. It has passed laws to protect large whale species. Unfortunately, the commission has more power over the welfare of larger species than smaller ones, like dolphins and porpoises.

What is CITES?

CITES (the Convention on International Trade in Endangered Species) was created in the 1960s to protect species that are threatened by international trade. Two lists classify dolphins and whales as either endangered or highly endangered.

Official U.S. Navy Photograph

◄ Since all countries have not agreed to the CITES restrictions, the treaty cannot fully protect animals like this Beluga.

Are there other laws to protect dolphins?

Many effective laws have been enforced within countries on a national level. The United States' Marine Mammal Protection Act (MMPA) is used by several states to create their own conservation programs. MMPA was designed specifically to deal with the death of dolphins in the nets of tuna-fishing companies.

► The Bottlenose Dolphin's playful spirit and "smiley" face make it a favorite of whale watchers.

By Thomas Jefferson

DOLPHIN SPECIES

By Michael W. Newcomer

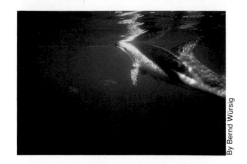

By Bernd Würsig

By Mari A. Smultea

▲ Lively, playful animals, Pacific White-Sided Dolphins leap high out of the water as they swim.

Pacific White-Sided Dolphin

The Pacific White-Sided Dolphin has a small beak, and a hooked dorsal fin. It weighs about 200 pounds (90kg) and grows to about 7 feet (2.1m) in length. Living in the deep temperate waters of the North Pacific Ocean, it can be found as far south as Baja California and in the Sea of Japan.

▲ Dusky Dolphins travel from shallow water to the open ocean each day to feed. Smaller herds of Duskies gather to form bigger herds in deeper water.

Dusky Dolphin

The Dusky Dolphin looks a lot like its cousin, the Pacific White-Sided Dolphin, but does not live in the same waters. It swims in the oceans off Argentina, New Zealand, and South Africa. Growing to a length of 6 feet (1.8m), it weighs 250 pounds (115kg). Its beak is very small.

▲The Hourglass Dolphin enjoys riding the waves when Antarctic seas turn stormy. It leaps and spins like an acrobat.

Hourglass Dolphin

This beautiful dolphin is named for the black and white hourglass-shaped markings on the sides of its body. Because it lives far away in Antarctic waters, its life is a mystery to scientists. Very few of these dolphins have ever been measured or weighed. The largest was a female measuring 6 feet (1.8m) and weighing 250 pounds (115kg).

By Michael W. Newcomer

▲ These fast-swimming dolphins live in groups of 500 or more. They keep to themselves, so they are difficult to study. Unlike many dolphins, Fraser's Dolphins never bow ride (see page 19).

Fraser's Dolphin

Until the early 1970s, nobody had ever seen any living Fraser's Dolphins. They are quite shy, and flee from approaching boats. No one knows how many there are, or what their babies are like. We do know that they grow to be about 8½ feet (2.6m) long, and that they weigh in at a hefty 460 pounds (209kg). Their flippers, flukes, and dorsal fins are rather small.

Spinner Dolphin

Spinner Dolphins are slim and trim. The largest are about 7 feet (2.1m) long and weigh 200 pounds (91kg). They live far from shore in tropical oceans around the world. Spinner Dolphins living in different parts of the world may not look alike. Some have hooked dorsal fins, while some others' fins are so straight, they look as if they are on backwards. Spinners have more teeth than any other dolphin (as many as 260), and a very long beak to keep them in!

▶The Spinner Dolphin lives in groups of up to 1,000 animals. Its favorite foods are squid and small fishes.

By Berrd Würsig

▲ Spinner Dolphins earn their names. You can see this one spinning as it leaps out of the water.

By Thomas Jefferson

By Thomas Jefferson

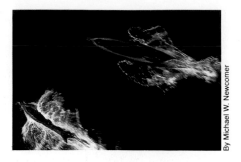

By Michael W. Newcomer

By Bernd Würsig

▲ The Common Dolphin can be found along the coast, but likes deep water the best. It may travel in herds of about 20 on up to several hundred.

Common Dolphin

This dolphin's black, grey, tan, and white markings make it one of the most colorful of all dolphins. The Common Dolphin grows to a length of 8 feet (2.1m) and weighs 165 pounds (75kg). It lives in temperate and tropical waters worldwide. The Common Dolphin eats smelt, herring, lanternfish, and squid. It hunts mostly at night.

Bottlenose Dolphin

The Bottlenose Dolphin is the largest of the "beaked" dolphins. It can grow to be nearly

▲ The Bottlenose Dolphin is probably the best known of all dolphins. It lives all over the world, except in the coldest waters. These two were photographed from the boat they were bow-riding.

13 feet (3.9m) long and may weigh over 600 pounds (275kg). Its back is grey, and its belly is light grey or pale pink. Some very unusual Bottlenose Dolphins are all white, black, or cinnamon colored. These dolphins work together to herd fish into a shallow spot where they are much easier to catch. Bottlenose Dolphins have been seen sliding up onto a beach after their panicking prey. They gulp the fishes down and then push themselves back into the water with their tails.

▲ The Rough-Toothed Dolphin looks quite a bit like the Bottlenose. These dolphins often swim together. It can be difficult to tell them apart out in the ocean.

Rough-Toothed Dolphin

The Rough-Toothed Dolphin has tiny wrinkles on its teeth, which make them feel rough. It is the only dolphin with a cone-shaped head. Its body is purplish black on top; its face and belly are blotchy white, pale yellow, and pink. It grows to 9 feet (2.7m) and weighs 350 pounds (160kg). It lives in mild temperate and tropical waters of the Pacific, Atlantic, and Indian oceans, and can also be found in the Gulf of Mexico.

Northern Right Whale Dolphin

This sleek dolphin's most distinctive feature is the lack of a dorsal fin. It has a slim body and a small beak. Except for its white chin and belly, it is shiny black. It is about 10 feet (3.1m) long and weighs 200 pounds (90kg). It lives in the North Pacific alongside the Pacific White-Sided Dolphin.

Killer Whale or Orca

The Orca is the largest dolphin. It can grow up to 31 feet (9.5m) and weigh 8 tons (7,200kg). This beautiful animal is black with a white belly. It has a white patch behind its eye, and a grey "saddle" patch behind its dorsal fin. Killer Whale pods remain together throughout their entire lives. Orcas live in tropical, temperate, and polar waters worldwide.

▶**The Orca's favorite foods are seabirds, turtles, fishes, sharks, whales, dolphins, porpoises, and seals.**

By Thomas Jefferson

▲**The Northern Right Whale Dolphin was named after the Right Whale, which also lacks a dorsal fin. These two cetaceans are not closely related. The Right Whale is a large baleen whale, not a dolphin.**

By Thomas Jefferson

Risso's Dolphin

The Risso's Dolphin has a stout body and no beak. It grows up to 13 feet (4m) long. The adult is light grey with a white belly and dark grey flippers and tail. Risso's Dolphins have fewer teeth than any other dolphin—only 6 to 14 teeth in the lower jaw, and none in the upper.

By Michael W. Newcomer

▲Older adults are covered with white scrapes and scratches made by the teeth of other Risso's Dolphins. Some of these scars may be made by the squid and octopuses that these dolphins eat.

By Michael W. Newcomer

◀Risso's Dolphins sometimes swim alone or in pairs, but you are more likely to see them in herds of 100 or more.

Vaquita

The name "Vaquita" is Spanish and means "little cow." This very rare porpoise lives only in the northern Gulf of California. Only a few Vaquita have been examined by scientists. The largest was just under 5 feet (1.5m) long. Of all the world's cetaceans, the little Vaquita is in the most danger of dying out.

▼ **Unfortunately, the best Vaquita pictures are of animals that have died. Mexican fishing boats are among the many dangers the little porpoise faces. This one died in a fishing net.**

By Michael W. Newcomer

By Michael W. Newcomer

▲ **If you look closely, you can see an adult and a baby Vaquita, the most endangered cetaceans in the world. This is one of the few pictures ever taken of a live Vaquita.**

Dall's Porpoise

This stocky porpoise grows to a length of 7 feet (2.2m) and weighs 480 pounds (220kg). Its body is black with a bold white belly patch, and its dorsal fin and flukes are edged in white or grey. The Dall's Porpoise is named after American scientist William Healey Dall, who first studied it in 1873.

By Michael W. Newcomer

▲ Found only in the North Pacific, the Dall's Porpoise travels in herds of 10 to 20. As many as 200 will gather if they find a large school of fish to eat.

By Michael W. Newcomer

▲ The Dall's Porpoise is the fastest and strongest swimmer of all cetaceans. It creates a splashing rooster tail as it cuts through the water's surface.

▶ The Dall's Porpoise is built for speed. Look at the muscular tail, slippery skin, and the sleek streamlined flukes. There is no faster mammal in the ocean.

Beiji or Chinese River Dolphin

According to a Chinese myth, a princess long ago drowned in the Yangtze River, and was re-born as a Beiji. This dolphin has been held sacred ever since. Of all the dolphins, the Beiji has lived the closest to humans. Now this is causing trouble for the Beiji, because it is no longer considered bad luck to kill it or disturb its home. The Beiji grows to a length of 8 feet (2.4m), and weighs up to 300 pounds (136kg). The female is usually larger than the male. This is rare among dolphins.

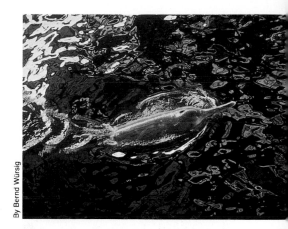

▲ Little is known about the Beiji. it is considered one of the 12 most endangered animals in the world.

Beluga

The Beluga is known as the "white whale." Although it is dark brown or bluish grey at birth, its color fades as it grows older and, by the time it reaches adulthood, it turns completely white. Instead of a dorsal fin, the Beluga has a "hump" on its back. It may grow up to 16 feet (5m) long and weigh up to 2,400 pounds (1,100kg). Belugas live in arctic and subarctic waters as well as in the Pacific and Atlantic oceans. The Beluga "chirps" when it is at the surface. This chirping has earned this whale the nickname "sea canary."

▲ Belugas can also be found in freshwater. These Belugas are swimming at the mouth of the MacKenzie River in the Yukon, Canada. Other Belugas live in the St. Lawrence River in Quebec, Canada.

▲ An unusual feature among cetaceans, the Beluga's flexible neck allows the animal to twist and turn its head.

Acknowledgements

We have many scientists and photographers to thank for their help with our book. It is no exaggeration to say that this project would have been impossible without them. Their devotion to their own callings has resulted in a storehouse of high-quality information and materials. They have selflessly shared this wealth with us, and we owe them everything. We cannot possibly do them justice in the space allowed, but we will give it our best.

Special thanks go to the Texas A&M University Marine Mammal Research Program in Galveston. Dr. Bernd Würsig, Dr. Graham Worthy, Thomas Jefferson, Barbara Curry, Jon Stern, Bill Stevens, and Terry Christopher donated their extraordinary photographs, edited text, and advised us throughout the entire project. We are indebted to Dagmar Fertl for her tireless efforts as liaison, coordinator, photographer and researcher.

Kathleen Dudzinski, with Oceanic Society Expeditions, has provided some of the loveliest spotted dolphin photos to be found anywhere. Mari A. Smultea, with the Pacific Whale Foundation, has done likewise with her outstanding humpback and pilot whales.

Thanks to Tom La Puzza, Public Affairs Officer, United States Navy, for his generous donation of beluga photographs.

The Texas Marine Mammal Stranding Network secured an entire bottlenose skeleton for us. Dr. Jim Hain, of Associated Scientists at Woods Hole, Inc., provided a fascinating right whale necropsy video. We cannot begin to express our gratitude for these materials.

Thanks to David Withrow, Robin Angliss, David Rugh, Dr. Howard Braham, and Sally Mizroch, of the National Marine Mammal Laboratory in Seattle, for their wonderful dolphin and whale slides and scientific reference.

Michael Philo at the Alaska Department of Wildlife Management sent us slides of the famous Point Barrow gray whale rescue. Dr. Wayne Vogl and David Pfeiffer at the University of British Columbia contributed some wonderful narwhal and beluga slides.

Our thanks also go out to Rocky Strong, Gene Kent, and Michael W. Newcomer.

Index